···A **TIMELINE HISTORY** OF THE··· TRAIL OF TEARS

··**TIMELINE TRACKERS**: WESTWARD EXPANSION··

ALISON BEHNKE

Lerner Publications ◆ Minneapolis

CONTENTS

Lerner Publications Company
A division of Lerner Publishing Group, Inc.
241 First Avenue North
Minneapolis, MN 55401 USA

For reading levels and more information, look up this title at www.lernerbooks.com.

Content consultant: Lloyd Arneach, Cherokee Storyteller, Member of the Eastern Band of Cherokee

Library of Congress Cataloging-in-Publication Data

Behnke, Alison.
   A timeline history of the Trail of Tears / Alison Marie Behnke.
     pages cm. — (Timeline trackers: westward expansion)
   Includes bibliographical references and index.
   Audience: Grades 4–6.
   ISBN 978-1-4677-8582-2 (lb : alk. paper)
   ISBN 978-1-4677-8640-9 (pb : alk. paper)
   ISBN 978-1-4677-8641-6 (EB pdf)
   1. Trail of Tears, 1838-1839—Juvenile literature.
2. Cherokee Indians—Relocation—Juvenile literature. 3. Cherokee Indians—History—Juvenile literature. I. Title.
E99.C5B375 2015
975.004'97557—dc23   2015000324

Manufactured in the United States of America
1 – BP – 7/15/15

COVER PHOTO:
The Cherokee people faced harsh and dangerous conditions on their forced journey west to the Indian Territory.

INTRODUCTION

In the early nineteenth century, the United States was growing quickly. But long before the young country existed, North America had been home to American Indians. Many different American Indian nations—separate self-governing groups—had lived on the land for centuries. One of the largest groups was the Cherokee. The Cherokee people lived in a region that would eventually become part of the southeastern United States.

Sometimes newcomers and American Indians interacted peacefully. They traded goods and shared information. Sometimes they fought alongside one another in battle. But often they came into conflict. And white Americans were hungry for the land on which American Indians lived.

These pressures built for many years. Eventually the US government made a major decision. With the Indian Removal Act of 1830, many American Indians in the Southeast were forced to move away from their homelands. In 1838 the Cherokee began a difficult and heartbreaking journey westward. Many people died. Those who survived had to start new lives, hundreds of miles from their homeland. The Cherokee called this tragic journey *Nunna daul isunyi*, or the Trail Where They Cried. In modern times, it is often referred to as the Trail of Tears.

TIMELINES

In this book, a series of dates and important events appear in timelines. Timelines are a visual way of showing a series of events over a time period. A timeline often reveals the cause and effect of events. It can help explain how one moment in history leads to the next. The timelines in this book display important turning points surrounding the Trail of Tears. Each timeline is marked with different intervals of time, depending on how close together events happened. Solid lines in the timelines indicate regular intervals of time. Dashed lines represent bigger jumps in time.

CHAPTER 1
AN ANCIENT HOMELAND

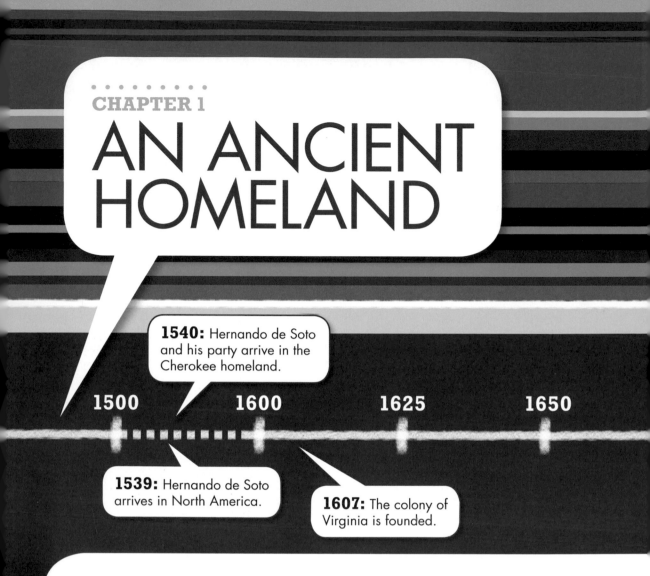

1540: Hernando de Soto and his party arrive in the Cherokee homeland.

1500   **1600**   **1625**   **1650**

1539: Hernando de Soto arrives in North America.

1607: The colony of Virginia is founded.

For centuries the Cherokee homeland was in the southern Appalachian Mountains. The borders shifted a little over the years. At one time or another, Cherokee land included parts of modern Kentucky, Tennessee, Georgia, Alabama, North Carolina, South Carolina, Virginia, and West Virginia.

While the Cherokee people sometimes had conflicts with neighbors, they also traded with other American Indians in the region. Other than the Cherokee, the largest groups in the area were the Choctaw, Chickasaw, Seminole, and Creek Indians.

Hundreds of years ago, the Cherokee people were not a single, organized group. They did not have a central government. Different villages mostly took care of their own affairs. But a shared language and history did unite them. The Cherokee called themselves Ani-Yunwiya. The name meant "the Real People."

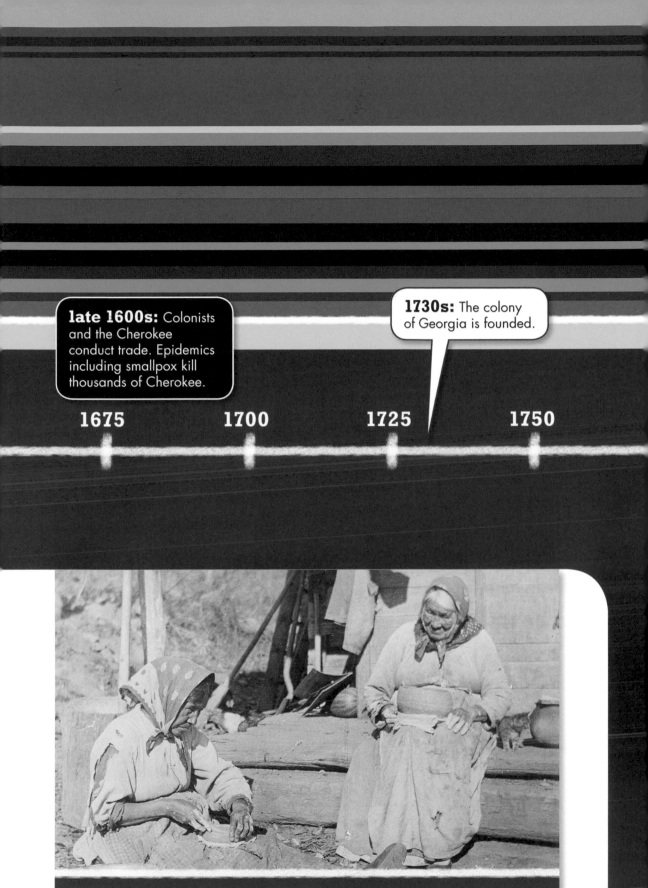

late 1600s: Colonists and the Cherokee conduct trade. Epidemics including smallpox kill thousands of Cherokee.

1730s: The colony of Georgia is founded.

1675   1700   1725   1750

Cherokee women make pottery from clay.

Cherokee life was centered on family and community. Extended families usually lived together in a village, along with members of other families. A typical Cherokee summer home was made of wood. In the winter, families moved into warmer homes with thick clay walls. The center of a village was the main plaza. On this plaza stood the town house, or council house. This building was where the Cherokee people gathered for special ceremonies, and it had seven sides so that each of the seven clans—traditional social groups of Cherokee society—would have their own place to sit. Village members also went to the town house to talk about important issues.

Within a Cherokee family, everyone had a role. Women owned the houses and were in charge of growing and gathering food. They also gathered wood to keep fires burning. They wove baskets from reeds and made pottery from clay.

Men and boys had different jobs. They made canoes out of

Modern demonstrations show how Cherokee canoes were made. A small fire softened the wood before the Cherokee used axes to carve and hollow out the tree trunks.

huge tree trunks. They crafted tools and weapons such as bows, arrows, and spears. Cherokee men and boys also hunted and fished. Families used the animals and fish for food and also for making tools and other items. Deerskins became clothes. Animal bones became arrowheads, fishhooks, and jewelry.

Like their daily lives, the Cherokee's spiritual beliefs were rooted in the place where they lived. Cherokee people had deep respect for the land and all it held, from mountains and sky to plants and animals. Cherokee people passed down many stories through the years to share their beliefs.

Cherokee life was not always easy. It was not completely peaceful. But despite occasional conflicts and hardships, the Cherokee people thrived in their bountiful homeland.

Then, in the mid-sixteenth century, Europeans reached Cherokee territory. For the Cherokee and other American Indians, that arrival would change their lives and futures forever.

Newcomers

In 1539 Spanish explorer Hernando de Soto arrived in North America. He led a group of about seven hundred people. They were looking for gold. De Soto was the first explorer to reach the Cherokee homeland.

CHEROKEE CLOTHING

Traditionally, Cherokee men wore long shirts, along with loincloths, leggings, and sometimes robes. Women wore dresses or skirts and blouses. Most clothes were made of deerskin or other animal hides. Sometimes they were also made of woven bark or plant fibers. Both men and women wore soft deerskin slippers called moccasins.

From 1539 through 1542, he and his party explored the region.

De Soto's group killed some of the American Indians they met. They took others prisoner. They forced these people to be their guides as they traveled west. In 1542 de Soto died. His group then headed south to Mexico.

Colonies and Conflict

The Cherokee people's first contact with Europeans was far from peaceful. After that, between the 1560s and the 1650s, the Cherokee did not see many more outsiders. Explorers were busy traveling to other parts of North and South America. English settlers were starting colonies north of the Cherokee homeland, such as the colony of Virginia. These colonies were ruled by England.

Hernando de Soto

As the number of settlers in the colonies grew, more colonists came in contact with American Indians. Sometimes American Indians helped the colonists with food or shelter. In some cases, the colonists and American Indians lived peacefully in the same region for a time.

But there were also conflicts. Throughout the colonies, settlers clashed with American Indians. Some American

Indians fled from the violence. They moved to more remote areas, farther from the colonial settlements. Others fought back. When they did, they were usually defeated by the settlers. The colonists had guns and other weapons that eventually overpowered many American Indian nations.

Over the years, many of these conflicts ended with treaties. These agreements often called for American Indians to follow laws set by the colonists. Sometimes they also required American Indians to sell or give away some of their land.

Colonists and American Indians also had positive interactions. Beginning in the late seventeenth century, trade was lively between English settlers and some groups of American Indians, including the Cherokee.

But the new arrivals also brought sickness. Europeans carried diseases that American Indians had never been exposed to. Smallpox was one of the deadliest. It killed many thousands of American Indians. Over time, the Cherokee population would grow again. But the diseases took a terrible toll.

Some meetings between American Indians and colonists were peaceful.

CHAPTER 2
POPULATION AND PRESSURES

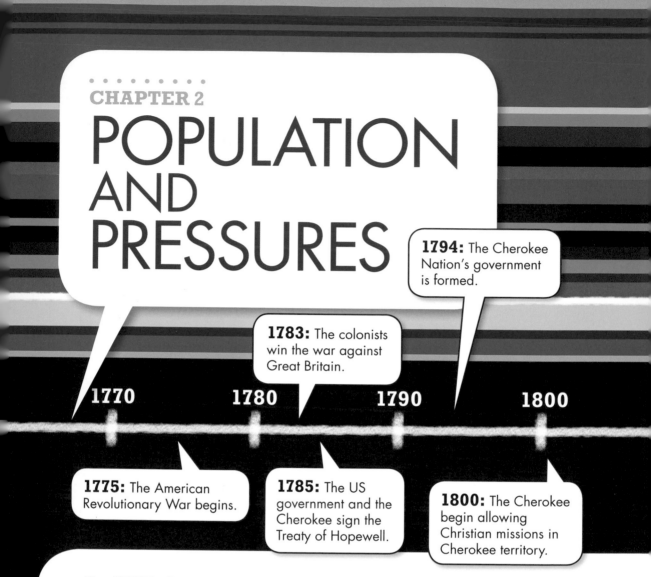

1794: The Cherokee Nation's government is formed.

1783: The colonists win the war against Great Britain.

1770 **1780** **1790** **1800**

1775: The American Revolutionary War begins.

1785: The US government and the Cherokee sign the Treaty of Hopewell.

1800: The Cherokee begin allowing Christian missions in Cherokee territory.

In 1775 the American Revolutionary War began. The North American colonists were fighting for their independence from Great Britain. During this war, members of some American Indian groups took sides. Some fought with the colonists. Others sided with the British. Most Cherokee chose to fight on the British side. In response, colonial soldiers attacked and destroyed some Cherokee towns.

In 1783 the colonists won their freedom. The United States was born from the revolution. Cherokee land fell within the new country's borders. The Cherokee and the US government signed the Treaty of Hopewell in 1785. The treaty defined the borders of Cherokee territory. It also said that if US citizens settled on land within that territory, the Cherokee had the right to use force to make those settlers leave.

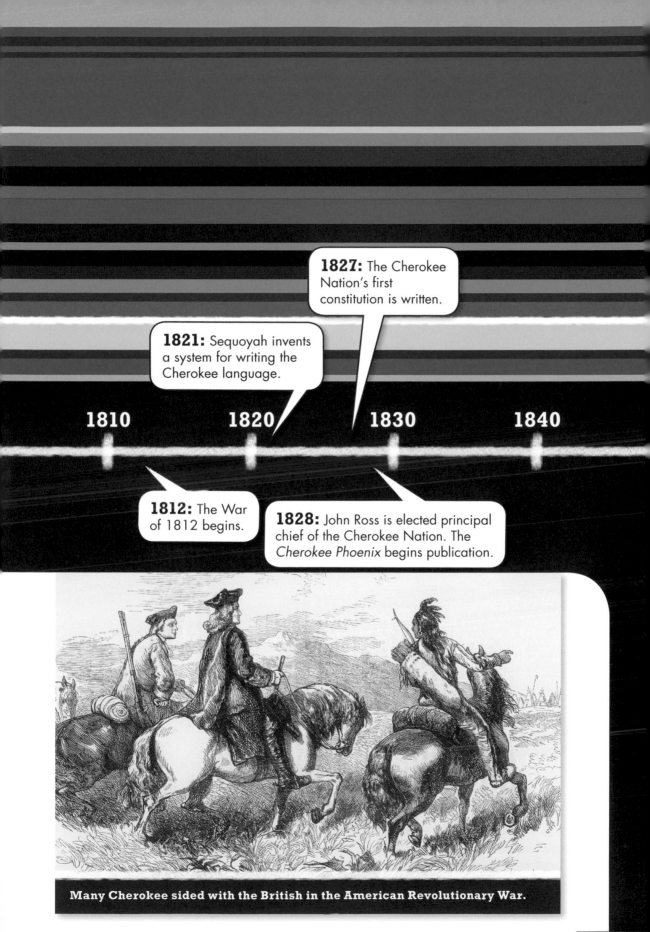

1827: The Cherokee Nation's first constitution is written.

1821: Sequoyah invents a system for writing the Cherokee language.

1810 1820 1830 1840

1812: The War of 1812 begins.

1828: John Ross is elected principal chief of the Cherokee Nation. The *Cherokee Phoenix* begins publication.

Many Cherokee sided with the British in the American Revolutionary War.

An Appetite for Land

The young United States grew quickly. At that time, the country was very different from its modern shape and size. But it soon added more territory. This expansion continued steadily, moving southward and westward.

US citizens were hungry for more land to settle. They put pressure on American Indians to sell their land or move away. Conflicts and disagreements over land continued. In response, the US government signed more treaties with the Cherokee and other American Indians. Most of these treaties required American Indians to sell land to the government. In return, these nations got money or goods.

Settlers eagerly moved onto land that the Cherokee had sold. And they didn't stop there. They pushed farther, moving across the borders into Cherokee territory and settling on land that didn't belong to them. Cherokee people sometimes fought back against this settlement. Some of these clashes became violent.

Early US citizens and Cherokee people often fought over land.

The Cherokee called on the US government to keep its promise to defend Cherokee territory. Meanwhile, US settlers and states demanded that the government protect them from Cherokee attacks. National leaders tried to solve the problem with even more treaties. Like earlier treaties, these agreements usually exchanged land for money. But the United States did not always enforce treaty terms, allowing settlers to push beyond the latest boundaries. This pattern continued for years.

While these arguments over land took place, a bigger discussion was going on. US leaders disagreed on the best way to handle the country's relationship with American Indian nations, especially in the Southeast. And many American Indians were torn about how to deal with European Americans. Could these very different cultures learn to live together?

The Call for Removal

One of the main ideas for addressing the situation was removal. Supporters of this idea wanted access to land held by the Cherokee and other southeastern nations. Advocates of removal wanted these nations to move west of the existing US states. Many believed American Indians were inferior to white people. Racism was common in the United States. White Americans often discriminated against people with darker skin.

Some US citizens did believe that the Cherokee had the right to stay on their land and that they should also be able to live as they wished. But this group was smaller than other groups calling for changes.

Pushing for Assimilation

Supporters of removal were one major voice in the debate about American Indians. Other voices in the debate called for assimilation. These people believed that American Indians should adopt ways of life more like those of white Americans.

For people in favor of this plan, a big part of assimilation was Christianity. For centuries, European settlers had been establishing missions aimed at converting American Indians to Christianity. In 1800 the Cherokee first allowed Christians to open a mission in their territory. In the years that followed, several branches of Christianity set up other missions among the Cherokee as well as among other American Indians in the Southeast. These posts sometimes included churches. But most Cherokee were more interested in the schools the missionaries founded. Teachers at these schools taught

Cherokee children who attended missionary-run schools were instructed in Christianity and white American customs as well as academic subjects.

Cherokee children to read and write in English. They also taught math. The Cherokee believed this education was very valuable. However, children were often punished severely if they were caught speaking their own language or practicing a Cherokee ceremony.

Teachers at the mission schools also worked to educate the Cherokee—young and old—about white customs and habits. For instance, Cherokee women traditionally grew crops. But white settlers believed that men should do the farmwork. The missionaries also wanted the Cherokee and other American Indians to become Christians.

Missionaries were not the only white citizens working among the Cherokee and other nations of the region. The US government also set up a Bureau of Indian Affairs. It hired officials called Indian agents. The bureau sent these agents to live near the Cherokee and other American Indians. The agents worked to keep peace between American Indians and settlers. And like the missionaries, they encouraged the Cherokee and other American Indians to adopt white customs.

Brainerd, a mission in Tennessee

Many Cherokee embraced the education offered by missionaries. Some did become Christians, but many others did not. At the same time, they resisted giving up parts of their culture. They held on to some of their own customs, such as traditional holidays and celebrations, as well as the Cherokee language.

Some of the changes adopted by Cherokee people were useful to their community. But others had negative results. For example, Cherokee women traditionally owned their homes and had a strong voice in their families and villages. But in white culture at the time, women had very few rights. They were

ROMANCE AND RACISM

Some Cherokee sought out education at schools far beyond the missions. For example, cousins Elias Boudinot (previously known as Young Buck before he moved to Connecticut) and John Ridge went to a school in Cornwall, Connecticut. But higher education did not protect these Cherokee from prejudice. While in Cornwall, Ridge met and fell in love with a young white woman named Sarah Bird Northrup. In 1824 the couple got married. In 1826 Boudinot (*upper right*) became engaged to Harriet Gold (*lower right*), another local white woman. Both couples faced anger and criticism for their relationships. Many US citizens disapproved of marriages between white people and American Indians or other people of color.

not allowed to vote or own property. They were also expected to obey the wishes of their husbands, fathers, or brothers. For Cherokee women, assimilation brought new hardships.

The Cherokee Nation

The nations of the Southeast largely embraced assimilation. The Cherokee, the Chickasaw, the Choctaw, the Creek, and the Seminole all began copying European-American ways of life. But the Cherokee went further than any other nation.

Cherokee leaders worked to form a more central government based on the US government system. This new system united a loosely connected group of independent communities to form the Cherokee Nation. Starting in 1794, the Cherokee Nation's government was led by a principal chief, whose role was similar to that of the US president. The government also included a legislature called the National Council. The Cherokee elected these leaders, who worked to make important decisions affecting the Cherokee Nation. Cherokee leaders created a police force and set up a justice system based on US institutions.

These changes somewhat improved relations between the Cherokee and the United States during the early nineteenth century. The Cherokee even aided the United States in several conflicts. For example, the United States fought the War of 1812 (1812–1815) against Great Britain over rights to territory and trade. Some American Indians joined forces with the British. Most Cherokee who took part fought for the United States.

Another important development to Cherokee life was the creation of a Cherokee writing system. Until then, the Cherokee people had not had a written language. They passed down legends, shared news, and taught customs in spoken words and through art. But times were changing. A Cherokee man named Sequoyah believed that a written language would help the Cherokee preserve their culture and spread information. When Sequoyah first had this idea, he did not know how to read or write in English or any other language. But he set out to change the way Cherokee people communicated.

Sequoyah

In 1821 Sequoyah finished creating a writing system for the Cherokee language. This work had taken him about twelve years. The system was called a syllabary. It used a symbol to represent each syllable in the language. Sequoyah began teaching his system to the people in his village. People who spoke the Cherokee language were able to learn to read and write using the syllabary very quickly. Before long, more and more Cherokee villages were learning it.

Using Sequoyah's invention, Cherokee leaders wrote the Cherokee Nation's first constitution in 1827. The document was modeled on the US Constitution. The following year, John Ross was elected as the Cherokee Nation's principal chief.

On February 21, 1828, the National Council also began publishing a newspaper called the *Cherokee Phoenix*. The paper printed articles in English as well as in the Cherokee language. The *Phoenix* printed articles and essays about Cherokee news, politics, and culture.

From the Cherokee legislature to the *Phoenix*, the nation seemed to be the model of assimilation. Yet despite that success at assimilation, pressure for removal remained. Many Cherokee wondered: Would assimilation really allow them to stay in their homeland?

The *Cherokee Phoenix* was printed in both English and the Cherokee language.

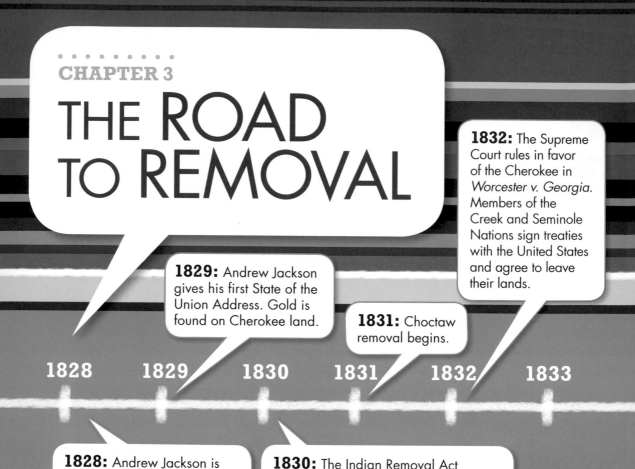

CHAPTER 3

THE ROAD TO REMOVAL

1832: The Supreme Court rules in favor of the Cherokee in *Worcester v. Georgia*. Members of the Creek and Seminole Nations sign treaties with the United States and agree to leave their lands.

1829: Andrew Jackson gives his first State of the Union Address. Gold is found on Cherokee land.

1831: Choctaw removal begins.

| 1828 | 1829 | 1830 | 1831 | 1832 | 1833 |

1828: Andrew Jackson is elected president. Georgia passes a law seriously limiting the rights of Cherokee people.

1830: The Indian Removal Act becomes law. The Choctaw of Mississippi sign a treaty with the United States and agree to leave their lands.

In December 1828, Andrew Jackson was elected as US president. Jackson was already a famous figure in the country. He had a history of taking part in US wars against American Indians. He had been an officer in the Creek War (1813–1814). In 1817 he was a key figure in the First Seminole War (1817–1818), in which the United States fought against the Seminole Nation in Florida.

After those conflicts, Jackson had helped create treaties with defeated American Indian nations. For example, after the Creek War, he insisted on a treaty that forced the Creek to give up huge amounts of land for a fairly small amount of money. And throughout his career, Jackson had supported the idea of removal. For most American Indian nations, his election was cause for alarm.

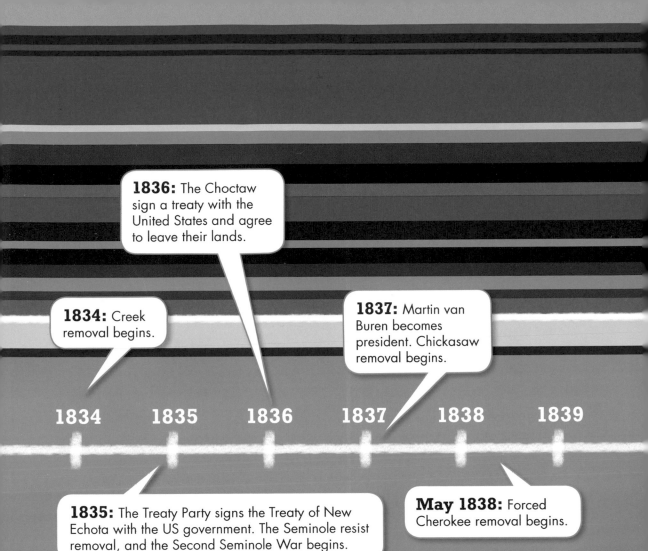

1836: The Choctaw sign a treaty with the United States and agree to leave their lands.

1834: Creek removal begins.

1837: Martin van Buren becomes president. Chickasaw removal begins.

1834   1835   1836   1837   1838   1839

1835: The Treaty Party signs the Treaty of New Echota with the US government. The Seminole resist removal, and the Second Seminole War begins.

May 1838: Forced Cherokee removal begins.

Setting the Stage

Jackson soon gave American Indians reasons to worry about his plans. In December 1829, the president delivered his first State of the Union Address. In the speech, he focused on the American Indians living in the Southeast. He claimed that the American Indian nations located within state borders had no right to form their own governments. Those nations, he said, should be controlled by the states where they lived. But he also noted that this situation threatened American Indians' survival.

Jackson believed that the only answer was removal. He proposed setting aside land west of the Mississippi River for American Indians to live on. This land would not be part of any existing US state or territory. There, Jackson said, the American Indians would be able to govern themselves.

US citizens would be able to claim the newly emptied eastern lands.

Jackson also said that the southeastern nations should be able to choose whether they moved. But if they stayed, they had to agree to follow the laws of the states where they lived.

American Indians in the Southeast faced a difficult choice. Leaving behind their homelands was a painful and scary thought. But staying behind presented big problems too. Most Cherokee did not want to give up the customs they'd followed for generations. But fitting in as citizens of US states would often require them to do just that.

In addition, some state laws severely limited American Indians' rights. For example, in late 1828, Georgia had passed a law saying that the state was taking over Cherokee territory within Georgia's borders. The law also stated that the Cherokee Nation's laws and

President Andrew Jackson

government were no longer legal in Georgia. And it said that while white citizens could charge Cherokee people with crimes, Cherokee people could not testify in court against white citizens. The law would go into effect June 1, 1830. Alabama passed a similar law in 1829.

Meanwhile, US citizens were more eager than ever to claim Cherokee territory. In 1829 gold had been found on Cherokee land within Georgia's state borders. Georgia's legislature also made it illegal for the Cherokee to mine or pan for gold on their own land. And the state government went even further. Georgia divided up Cherokee territory and allowed white Georgians to buy plots of land. The Cherokee were in danger of losing their homeland even if they refused to move elsewhere.

A Historic Debate

In early 1830, Jackson drafted a law called the Indian Removal Act. The act described a region that could serve as the "Indian Territory." In modern times, this land is mostly within Oklahoma. The area would be split into sections for each of the nations moving west.

Jackson's act also said that the US government would trade this western land for land the American Indians left behind. So the more territory a group had in the East, the more it would get in the West. In addition, the government would pay the cost of the journey westward.

US citizens search for gold on Cherokee land.

In April 1830, the act went to Congress for debate. Congress needed to approve the bill for it to become law. The debate was heated. Lawmakers and other US citizens were divided on the issue.

Some believed that forcing American Indians out of their homes was deeply unfair. One person who opposed the act was missionary Jeremiah Evarts. Evarts had lived and worked among the Cherokee and other American Indians. Evarts said it was cruel to force American Indians to leave their homes. He also pointed out that the United States had signed treaties promising to protect the Cherokee people from settlers taking their land. Evarts and others felt that the United States was wrong to ignore these treaties.

The Indian Removal Act was heavily debated in Congress.

Other people felt sympathy for the American Indians but still supported removal. These people said that the Cherokee and other American Indians would only suffer as white settlers moved into their homelands. According to these supporters of removal, the Cherokee would be better off in the Indian Territory.

Still other US citizens were prejudiced against American Indians. They believed that American Indians did not deserve the same rights as white people. These people thought that white settlers had a greater right to own the land.

After more than two weeks of debate, the Senate voted to pass the bill. The bill then went to the House of Representatives. There, debate took thirteen days. At last, the House passed the bill by a close vote of 102 to 97. On May 28, 1830, Jackson signed the bill into law.

Working for Change

American Indians in the Southeast were deeply upset that the Indian Removal Act had passed. Some nations, hoping to avoid more conflict, quickly agreed to sell their lands and move. But for many others, this was not the end of the struggle to stay in their homeland. Instead, they started thinking of ways to fight the law.

In 1831 Cherokee leaders took a legal case to the Supreme Court. In *Cherokee Nation v. Georgia*, Cherokee leaders and their lawyers asked the Supreme Court to order Georgia not to enforce the new laws limiting Cherokee rights. The court's judges reviewed the case. But they did not agree to issue an order to Georgia.

The Cherokee Nation tried again in 1832 with *Worcester v. Georgia*. This time, the Supreme Court ruled in favor of the Cherokee. The court said that the Cherokee Nation had the right to govern itself. Therefore, Georgia's laws limiting that power were not valid.

However, when Georgia officials ignored the court's decision, President Jackson made no effort to enforce the ruling. Instead, he kept pushing hard for removal. By 1835 his plan was succeeding elsewhere in the Southeast. Most other major nations had given in to US pressure and signed treaties selling their land. The Choctaw of Mississippi had already moved west. So had the Creek—who had already lost most of their lands after the Creek War and had been living in a small region of Alabama. The Seminole of Florida resisted removal with violence. But even as the Second Seminole War (1835–1842) raged, the US government did not forget the Cherokee. Removal supporters believed it was only a matter of time before US policy succeeded.

Disagreements and Decisions

Meanwhile, divisions had appeared among the Cherokee people. And those divisions were getting deeper. Most Cherokee wanted to keep working for a way to stay in their homeland. Chief John Ross was the leader of this group, sometimes called the National Party.

But a smaller group with different ideas began to form. These people urged others to prepare for removal. It was clear, they said, that Georgia and other states wanted the Cherokee out. And, they added, those states would only make life harder for the Cherokee the longer the Cherokee stayed put.

One Cherokee who accepted the idea of removal was Major Ridge. Ridge was an influential figure in the Cherokee Nation. He believed that the only way to protect the Cherokee was to agree to leave the homeland. Ridge and his followers were called the Treaty Party. They hoped to make a good deal with the government before it was too late.

John Ross tried to unite the Cherokee people in resisting removal and rejecting the Treaty Party. He gave speeches. He wrote articles for the *Cherokee Phoenix*. And he talked with US government officials about other options. But Ross couldn't stop members of the Treaty Party from making their own trips to Washington, DC. In the capital, Ridge and others met with US leaders about possible removal deals.

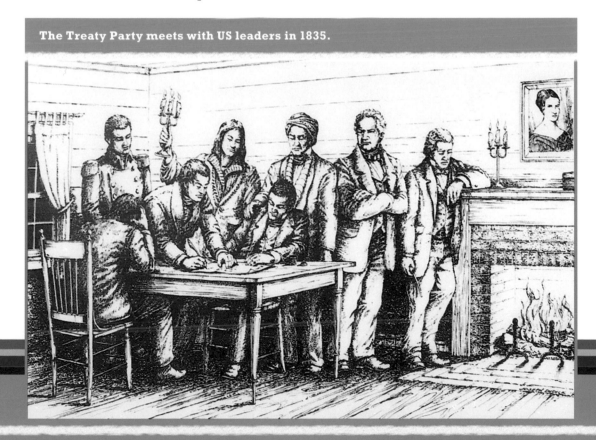
The Treaty Party meets with US leaders in 1835.

Jackson and his supporters were happy to work with the Treaty Party. They wanted to create an agreement that would lock in a plan for removal. On December 29, 1835, they succeeded. Ridge and some of the Treaty Party members signed the Treaty of New Echota. The signers numbered fewer than two hundred Cherokee—a tiny part of the Cherokee Nation's population. But they made a decision that affected all Cherokee people.

The treaty said that the Cherokee would give up their lands in exchange for $5 million from the US government. The Cherokee would also get money for homes and other property left behind. And once American Indians reached the Indian Territory, the government would give them money to set up schools and to buy food for one year. The treaty also said that once the US Congress approved the agreement, the Cherokee people would have two years to move. After that, US officials would have the right to force them out.

Congress signed the treaty in May 1836 after approving it by only one vote. The date of forced removal was set: May 23, 1838.

OLD AND NEW

Some Cherokee people had already moved west before the debate about removal heated up. Beginning in the late eighteenth century and lasting into the early nineteenth century, smaller groups of a few hundred or a few thousand Cherokee sold their territory through treaties and left the Southeast. These early migrants to Indian Territory became known as the Old Settlers.

The Journey Begins

After the Treaty of New Echota, some groups of Cherokee started heading west immediately. Members of the Treaty Party were among the first to leave. But even for those who supported removal, the journey was difficult. Saying good-bye to the Cherokee homeland was painful. And the trip to Indian Territory was long and often dangerous. For some travelers, it ended in disaster. A group of 365 left in October 1837. It took them more than two months to reach Indian Territory. The group suffered cold weather and sickness. Fifteen people died. Most of the dead were children.

In the two years after the Treaty of New Echota, about two thousand Cherokee moved to the Indian Territory. All the

Chief John Ross

while, Chief John Ross kept trying to convince US leaders to give the nation more time and to avoid using force. By then Andrew Jackson's presidency was over. In March 1837, Martin van Buren had become president. Some people hoped that the new president would bring new policies. But van Buren did not change Jackson's plans. And while Ross kept fighting, time kept passing.

CHAPTER 4

THE TRAIL OF TEARS AND BEYOND

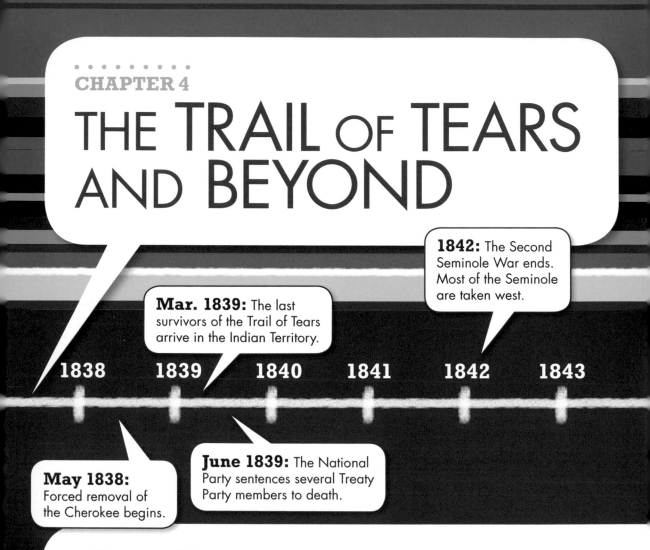

1842: The Second Seminole War ends. Most of the Seminole are taken west.

Mar. 1839: The last survivors of the Trail of Tears arrive in the Indian Territory.

1838   1839   1840   1841   1842   1843

June 1839: The National Party sentences several Treaty Party members to death.

May 1838: Forced removal of the Cherokee begins.

The deadline for Cherokee removal arrived on May 23, 1838. Before then US officials knew that most of the Cherokee would not choose to leave. Seven thousand men—most of them soldiers—had been gathering in the Southeast. The US military also set up thirty-one forts in the territory the Cherokee were being forced to leave.

"The Soldiers Came"

The military officer in charge of removal was General Winfield Scott. He hoped to carry out removal as peacefully as possible. He ordered his soldiers to be kind to the Cherokee people. Scott also worried that the Cherokee might rebel.

On May 10, Scott took command of the removal. He met

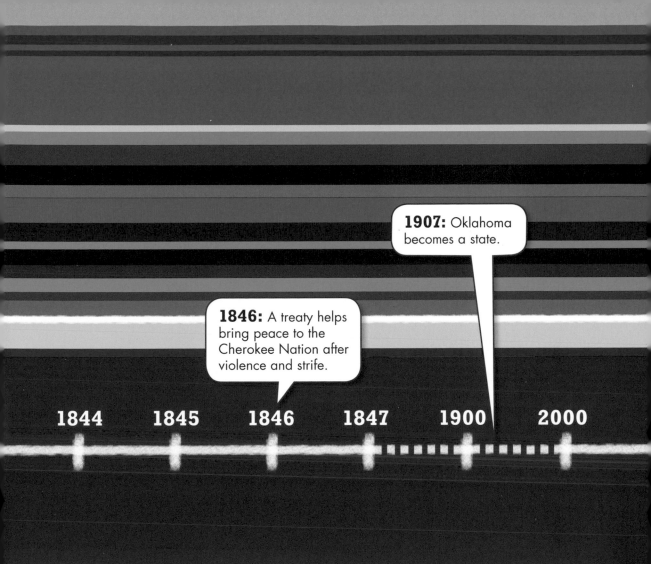

1907: Oklahoma becomes a state.

1846: A treaty helps bring peace to the Cherokee Nation after violence and strife.

1844   1845   1846   1847   1900   2000

with Cherokee leaders and urged them to go without a fight, warning them that he led a powerful army. He told them that his men were prepared to use force. But he also claimed that they would not do so unless needed.

That month, Scott's troops began rounding up the Cherokee. They forced people out of their homes. Until then many Cherokee had still been holding on to hope that removal would be delayed. So most families had not packed their belongings ahead of time. When the deadline did arrive, soldiers often gave the Cherokee little time to prepare. Some of the roundups happened so quickly that soldiers didn't let people pack clothes or other basic goods. A Cherokee woman named Ooloocha later told the story of her family's removal. She remembered, "The soldiers came and took us from home.

They first surrounded our house . . . while we were at work in the fields and they drove us out of doors and did not permit us to take anything with us."

As a result, many Cherokee people suddenly found themselves in poverty. In addition to their houses, they had lost horses, tools, clothes, and other possessions. Even as Cherokee people faced these losses, the revolt that Scott feared did not happen. Most Cherokee, surrounded by well-armed soldiers, believed it was hopeless to resist.

In spite of this, some soldiers did not display the kindness Scott had promised. Some of Scott's men even taunted the people they were taking prisoner. In addition, Scott had ordered that very sick people would not have to be moved yet. But some soldiers ignored this order.

Citizens of the states American Indians were leaving took advantage of the situation. In Georgia, as the military rounded up Cherokee families, white people stole from empty homes and even burned them down. Some reports said that Georgians dug up graves, looking for jewelry that had been buried with the dead.

Some soldiers did not let Cherokee people pack clothes or other essential belongings.

The Terrible Wait

The military forced Cherokee people into stockades after rounding them up. Most stockades were built inside forts the US military had set up in Cherokee territory. Imprisoned Cherokee families lived in these stockades while they waited to be moved westward. Many people were crowded into small spaces. They were not free to leave. People had almost no privacy in these close quarters. Sickness spread very quickly.

Most Cherokee did not stay at the forts very long. Space was limited. And about twenty thousand Cherokee were being forced west. So soldiers moved people from the forts to camps. Like the forts, these camps had been built by the US military. From there, groups would set off on the trip to Indian Territory.

Conditions at the camps were not much better. Some Cherokee people died at the camps. And the journey from the forts to the camps could be difficult. As they traveled to camps, Cherokee families often had to sleep on the ground without shelter.

The military removed Cherokee people from their homes and forced them into cramped stockades built inside forts.

In June the military started gathering the first large group of Cherokee to make the trip to Indian Territory. This group of almost three thousand Cherokee was split into three smaller groups. Some boarded boats on the Tennessee River. Others went by train at first. And others traveled in wagons or on horseback, but there were not enough wagons. Most Cherokee in this group were forced to make the journey on foot. Meanwhile, thousands of other Cherokee remained in the camps, still waiting.

For those who set out for the West that summer, the journey was brutal. It was a long trip—about 800 miles (1,287 kilometers). And the summer was very hot. Water was hard to find along the route to the Indian Territory. Dozens of Cherokee died.

After that first group's journey, John Ross was afraid that many more Cherokee would die unless he stepped in. He talked to Scott about the danger and the suffering. And he convinced US officials that it would be best for the Cherokee to be in charge of their own removal. They would still have to follow a timeline that the US government set. And the US military would still make sure the removal took place. The

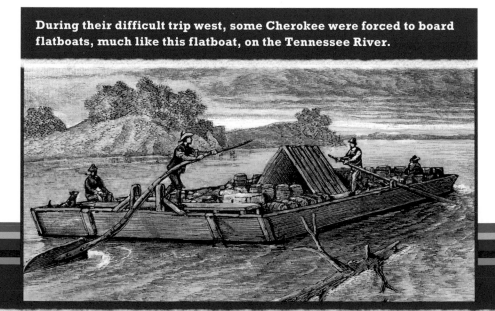

During their difficult trip west, some Cherokee were forced to board flatboats, much like this flatboat, on the Tennessee River.

government also provided wagons, horses, and oxen. But Ross's plan let the Cherokee make decisions about how to organize the groups and when to travel.

Ross prepared his people as well as he could. He arranged travel parties of about one thousand each. Ross also worked to set aside food and other goods for safe journeys.

On the Trail

As the groups organized by Ross set out, they traveled with wagons. Oxen, mules, or horses pulled these vehicles. There was one wagon for every eighteen people or so. But the wagons weren't big enough to fit that many people. So some Cherokee rode on horseback, and the vast majority walked. Often they carried the few belongings they'd saved. On average, a day's journey was 10 to 15 miles (16 to 24 km).

Travel time to the Indian Territory varied depending on the route, the weather, and other factors. One early group who went before the May 23 deadline traveled mostly by boat.

The Cherokee traveled to Indian Territory on foot, on horseback, and by wagon.

They had a fairly smooth trip of less than a month. But for others, the journey took more than three months.

Thousands of Cherokee people died along the trail. Some were already sick after catching illnesses in the camps. Others fell ill along the way. Common diseases included dysentery, measles, and whooping cough. Harsh weather made it harder for the healthy to stay well and for the sick to recover. Days could be hot, while nights were often cold. And because the military had rounded up the Cherokee during the summer, people lacked the warm clothes they needed for autumn and winter.

As autumn wore on, the travelers often faced sleet and snow. At night, groups of Cherokee often had to pitch tents or sleep in the small number of wagons. Some slept outside with no shelter. Food was sometimes scarce or of poor quality. And finding clean water to drink could be a challenge. Due to these harsh conditions, thousands of Cherokee buried family and friends along the trail in shallow graves. One of the graves held John Ross's wife, Quatie. According to stories from the trail, Quatie Ross was ill. But she gave the blanket covering her shoulders to a sick child. The next day, she died.

In the winter of 1839, the last

Quatie Ross

group of Cherokee people reached the Indian Territory. The survivors had endured terrible hardships. An estimated four thousand Cherokee had died—about one-fourth of the people who began the trip. Most of those who died were children and the elderly.

Even some of the survivors died soon after arrival. The trip had weakened many people. New outbreaks of disease ripped through the community in Indian Territory.

Decades later, a soldier from Georgia recalled the Trail of Tears with sorrow. He said, "I fought through the Civil War and have seen men shot to pieces and slaughtered by thousands, but the Cherokee removal was the cruelest work I ever knew."

One final group of Cherokee settlers endured snow and cold as they traveled from their homeland to the Indian Territory in the winter of 1839.

Starting Over

Starting over in the West was very hard. After the difficult journey, the Cherokee faced new challenges. For example, people who arrived with the later groups did not get very good plots of land. The best farmland had already been taken by earlier arrivals. And because people had left so many things behind, most did not have good tools or animals for farming.

Other problems also cropped up. Tensions were rising between the new arrivals and the Old Settlers—Cherokee who had come west before the forced removal. These groups had different ideas for the Cherokee Nation's government. And the divisions opened by the removal debate had not healed. Many Cherokee were very angry with the Treaty Party, whom they saw as traitors. The Cherokee had a law that anyone who sold Cherokee land without approval of the National Council would be executed. In June 1839, members of the National Party had sentenced several Treaty Party members to death for their part in the Treaty of New Echota. Further violence broke out as disagreements among the Old Settlers, the Treaty Party, and the National Party continued.

Major Ridge of the Treaty Party

The years between 1839 and 1846 were full of discord. But in 1846, a treaty within the Cherokee Nation finally brought peace.

All the while, most Cherokee tried to begin new lives in a new land. They built new schools and homes. They worked hard to raise crops. They once again published a newspaper, the *Cherokee Advocate*. John Ross continued talking to US leaders. He was working to protect Cherokee rights in their new land. He also wanted to make sure the Cherokee Nation was paid the money the US government had promised.

As the years passed, the United States kept expanding westward. US settlers continued their push onto new lands. Once again, the Cherokee faced huge pressure from the US government to sell away their lands, bit by bit. Then, in 1907, Oklahoma became a state. The Indian Territory was no more. But the Cherokee Nation continued. It still exists in the modern United States. It is no longer a physical nation with geographical borders. Yet it is an organized, recognized government.

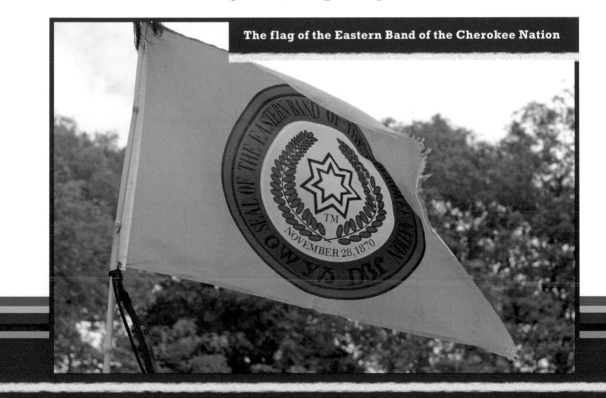
The flag of the Eastern Band of the Cherokee Nation

The Cherokee Nation's capital is Tahlequah, Oklahoma. It has more than 317,000 citizens, most living in Oklahoma. Two other main Cherokee groups also exist. The Eastern Band of Cherokee Indians is based in North Carolina. This group descended from a small group of around one thousand Cherokee people who had been allowed to stay in North Carolina. Their numbers grew when they were joined by Cherokee people who had escaped into hiding in the mountains before removal. The other main group is the United Keetoowah Band of Cherokee Indians. Centered in Oklahoma, these Cherokee people are mostly descended from the Old Settlers.

MANY TEARS

When people use the term "Trail of Tears," they are usually talking about the Cherokee removal. However, the term can also apply to other forced removals of American Indian nations during the 1830s. The Choctaw were the first large southeastern nation to leave after the Indian Removal Act became law. Their removal took place in three waves. First, a group of about four thousand went west in October 1831. The rest followed in 1832 and 1833. An estimated one out of five people died along the way. The causes of death included starvation, cholera, and bitter cold. A newspaper reporter for the *Arkansas Gazette* interviewed a Choctaw leader after removal. The leader called the journey "a trail of tears and death." The Creek went next, between 1834 and 1837. And the Chickasaw traveled westward in 1837. Finally, the last large group of the Seminole went through removal in 1842. Each of these journeys brought suffering and sadness.

After the Trail of Tears, the Cherokee, like other displaced American Indian nations, rebuilt their communities and protected their culture. But the removal's scars can never be erased. Wilma Mankiller, who became the Cherokee Nation's first female principal chief in 1985, was not alive when the Cherokee journeyed on the Trail of Tears. Yet she warned her fellow Cherokee not to let it fade from the people's memory. "It is so crucial for us to focus on the good things—our tenacity [determination], our language and culture, the revitalization of tribal communities," she wrote in 1993. But, she went on, "It is also important that we never forget what happened to our people on the Trail of Tears."

Wilma Mankiller

Writing Activity

Imagine that you are a Cherokee on the Trail of Tears. How would this experience affect you? How would it affect your family? Your larger community?

Choose an event from one of the timelines that interests you. Imagine that you saw or participated in this event. Then write a journal entry about this event. As you write, think about questions such as these:

How did you feel about the event?

What did you do in response to the event?

What surprised you most about this event?

How was your life different after this event?

What is the most important thing you want to remember about this event?

Source Notes

33–34 Theda Perdue and Michael D. Green, *The Cherokee Nation and the Trail of Tears* (New York: Penguin, 2008), 123–124.

39 David E. Stannard, *American Holocaust: The Conquest of the New World* (New York: Oxford University Press, 1992), 123.

42 A. J. Langguth, *Driven West: Andrew Jackson and the Trail of Tears to the Civil War* (New York: Simon & Schuster, 2010), 165–166.

43 Wilma Pearl Mankiller and Michael Wallis, *Mankiller: A Chief and Her People* (New York: St. Martin's, 1993), 48–49.

Glossary

assimilation: the process of making a person or a group of people behave more like another group of people

discriminate: to treat a person or people unfairly

missionary: a religious worker. Missionaries often work to convert people to a religion but may also build schools and do other community work.

nation: a self-governing group of people who usually share a culture

prejudice: an idea or an opinion (often negative) that is not based on reason or actual experience

stockade: a military prison

treaty: a written agreement between two or more parties

Further Information

Behnke, Alison. *A Timeline History of the Transcontinental Railroad*. Minneapolis: Lerner Publications, 2015. This book explores another aspect of US westward expansion that led to the displacement of American Indian peoples.

The Cherokee Nation
http://www.cherokee.org
This website has information about the modern Cherokee Nation, as well as details about Cherokee history, famous figures, and more.

Gimpel, Diane Marczely. *A Timeline History of Early American Indian Peoples*. Minneapolis: Lerner Publications, 2015. Learn about the lives and cultures of American Indians, including the Cherokee, before and after European settlers arrived in North America.

Josephson, Judith Pinkerton. *Why Did Cherokees Move West? And Other Questions about the Trail of Tears*. Minneapolis: Lerner Publications, 2011. This book includes many details about the dangerous and difficult 1,000-mile (1,609 km) journey the Cherokee people were forced to undertake to move to Indian Territory in Oklahoma.

LERNER
e
SOURCE

Expand learning beyond the printed book. Download free, complementary educational resources for this book from our website, www.lerneresource.com.

Index

Photo Acknowledgments

The images in this book are used with the permission of: © Herbert Tauss/National Geographic Image Collection/Alamy, p. 5; National Anthropological Archives, Smithsonian Institution, 1033, p. 7; © Marilyn Angel Wynn/Nativestock.com, p. 8; © Prisma/UIG/Getty Images, p. 10; © Gerry Embleton/North Wind Picture Archives, p. 11; © Print Collector/Getty Images, p. 13; The Granger Collection, New York, pp. 14, 17, 35, 38; courtesy of the Oklahoma Historical Society, pp. 16 (7706.N), 18 (19615.31); Wikimedia Commons (PD-US), p. 18 (top); Library of Congress, pp. 20 (LC-USZC4-2566), 26 (LC-DIG-ppmsca-09409), 31 (LC-USZC4-3156); The Beinecke Rare Book and Manuscript Library, Yale University, p. 21; painting by Ralph E. W. Earl, image courtesy of the White House/Wikimedia Commons (PD-US), p. 24; © North Wind Picture Archives, pp. 25, 36; Photo: Ed Jackson, p. 29; © Max D. Standley courtesy R. Michelson Galleries, pp. 34, 37; © Look and Learn Collection/Bridgeman Images, p. 39; © Smithsonian American Art Museum, Washington, DC /Art Resource, NY, p. 40; © Chris Cooper-Smith/Alamy, p. 41; © Peter Brooker/Rex Features/Presselect/Alamy, p. 43.

Front cover: Trail of Tears by Robert Lindneux, The Granger Collection, New York.

Main text font set in Caecilia Com 55 Roman 11/16.
Typeface provided by Linotype AG.